Knowing The Future
In Real Estate

~

...Which Way It's Headed
And How To Profit From It

by
Marty J. Reep

First edition.

Cover design courtesy of John Janecek.
Used with permission.

Disclaimer: The information in this book is for educational and entertainment purposes. It is not intended as legal advice. For that, consult a legal professional. Investing in anything can be risky.

ISBN-10: 1475100191
ISBN-13: 978-1475100198

To schedule Marty Reep to speak to your group or organization, please contact him via the information below:

MARTY J. REEP
Lompoc, California 93436
MartyJReep AT gmail DOT com
www.scribd.com/mjreep

To You,
because you want to learn and earn.

Thanks
to all the people who helped make this book
become a tangible reality by editing and
offering tangible suggestions:

Janet, Kristine, Whitt, and Cody.

Otherwise, this would still be bouncing around
inside my head, taking up space.

CONTENTS

FOREWORD

What would you think if I told you that you could know when the tops and bottoms of real estate prices will occur, _before_ they happen? *How much would it be worth to you? To your family? To your company?*

This book reveals that and more.

Hi, I'm Marty J. Reep, and this book is part of my continuously unfolding real estate story. It explains some of the things I've learned about cycles, tops, bottoms, and overall conditions of the real estate market.

I learned most of these things the hard way, and that's part of the reason I'm sharing them with you – so you don't have to go through the same financial roller coaster that I did in order to learn what's held within these pages. If some of the information can save you heartache, headaches, and/or wallet-ache, then I will have accomplished one of my goals.

In the United States, 2002-2007 was one of the biggest housing bubbles in history. A lot of people (who sold at the right time) made a lot of money –

and rightly so. I hope they're utilizing their gains, well.

On the other hand, people who bought those same houses (at the wrong time) may have lost a lot of money. I truly feel sorry for them.

No matter which side of that proverbial fence you find yourself on, I hope that this book will help you profit from real estate trends in the future.

When the idea of there being a repeating cycle in real estate occurred to me in 2005, I researched it, watched trends, watched prices, and then saw my predictions confirmed as they played out in front of my eyes.

Since then, I've taught my own kids how to read the graphs and watch trends. I've also taught them when the upcoming times would be best to buy and sell, because I figured that this knowledge wasn't just for me to know, but it was for them, as well.

However they're able to benefit from it will be up to them (and their children, one day), but it *is* my responsibility to make them aware of it and to walk them through the process.

Likewise, I'm sharing this information with you, because it's not just for me to know. A lot of people can benefit from it, so me being selfish about it wouldn't be right.

I hope that this information helps you to learn some new concepts and to have a few "ah-ha" moments as you read it.

Enjoy,

Marty

THE STORY

Where It Started

In December 2004, I bought a piece of property with plans to tear down the old house that was on it, subdivide the land, build two new houses, and sell both while the real estate market was still moving up. However, that's not how everything played out. Back then, I didn't realize that there was a definitive price cycle in real estate, nor how close to the top of it that I had bought my investment property.

With the development project, things seemed to moving along smoothly, from January to March, 2005. However, about April, I started running into obstacles with the local permitting offices in the county where the property was located. Apparently, five years of increased building permits had taken its toll on the little office that handled all of the paperwork, and the county put a big slowdown on the speed of getting paperwork in and out of the office, along with the timeframe in which they handled status inquiries.

Setback after setback occurred with the permit/loan/administrative process, and being new to "the construction/development game," I didn't know the right questions to ask in order to get the solutions I needed. Bureaucratic "red tape" was alive and annoying my finances.

About then, I started getting an uneasy feeling about the "train" I had gotten onto and wasn't quite sure what to do about it. So, I stuck it out and continued moving forward, hoping for the best.

Locals in the northwestern corner of California will tell you that weather during the winter and spring months can be touchy on good days and downright nasty on bad ones. But, like a friend of mine used to say, "Hang in there. We always dry out eventually."

The weather was overpowering from about November 2005 through March 2006 – it rained some 50 inches! So much water poured out of the sky that the ground was saturated for months.

Week after week, I just stared at the weather maps with my jaw dropped open. It was uncanny.

A couple of times, when I was talking with the contractor, he said that he had been tempted to go out and throw himself face down in the mud pit that was forming where the houses were to go. I told him he better not, because no construction project was anywhere close to being as important as his life! He was joking, but I understood the level of frustration he was trying to get across.

Yet, as I slogged through the permitting process, the red tape, and the uncooperative weather, I developed strong friendships with a few people who were working along with me on the building project.

Those connections are still intact, today, thank goodness!

While waiting for permits to process and praying for clear skies, I continued to read articles, books, and reports on real estate.

I was trying to make sense of the seemingly unending climb of property prices.

About then, I came across a real estate article about developer Tom Barrack. At the time, it seemed that he owned more U.S. commercial real estate than Donald Trump, and he was *GETTING OUT* of the U.S. market altogether.

Immediately, the weight of those words hit me – it was the top of the market, and the biggest player was cashing in his chips. He was like those guys at the stock market who ring the bell, signifying a new "all time high" for a market – and this guy was getting out.

"How did he know?"

Experience? Had he lived through a similar thing already and knew when to profit from it, this time?

"What did he know that I didn't?"

Apparently, plenty!

"How could I find out what he knew?"

Call him up… "Hey Mr. Real Estate Mogul who has an unlisted number…this is Marty Reep… Nah, you don't know me, but I need to pick your brain…trying to save my financial backside…Meet for lunch in Santa Barbara? Great – oh, and Trump's in town? Perfect!"

Maybe I *should have* called him...you never know!

What did happen, though, is that interview article caused me to research trends and cycles in real estate, like my life depended on it…because in some ways, it felt like it did! During the next few weeks, I started finding all kinds of research that other people had done on trends, cycles, real estate, correlation, causation, possibilities, flukes, and dead-on predictions.

A research trip to a university's library finally hit "pay dirt" for me: right there on the shelf was a book that opened my eyes to all sorts of possibilities, <u>Cycles: the Science of Prediction</u>, by Edward R.

Dewey and Edwin F. Dakin, published in 1947. Dewey and Dakin had laid out some cycles in real estate that made total sense.

After reading a few sections of the book, I started thinking, *"1947?! People have known about this stuff since 1947?! Why didn't I know this, before? Why didn't anybody tell me?"*

Those thoughts and others were racing through my mind.

I must have started talking to myself at some point, because when I looked up I realized that a college student was staring at me! I grinned, nodded, and kept reading.

As I read further in the book, that day, I realized that if I played out the expected cycles with real prices from 1947 until 2005, it would give me a good indication of how right-on-the-mark those guys were.

Graphing out the dates and numbers, I got a pretty good picture of how it all worked. Then, I started running the graph out into the future.

My eyes started getting big.

It was like having a "crystal ball" for prices in real estate. I told my wife what I thought that prices were going to do.

Her first response was a laughingly-smiled, "Huh? What are you talking about?"

I explained it, again, and showed her the books, along with my graphs.

Something clicked in her head, because she said, "Well, let's wait and see what happens."

Since then, reality has matched those predicting graphs.

Now, roll forward a year…

Discovering Hidden Cycles

During the summer and fall of 2006, I worked part time at a real estate loan office. Part of my job was to find people who needed loans and then match up the loans we could do, with their needs.

One day, my coworker, Vince, and I started talking about interest rates.

I asked him, "Wouldn't it be cool if we could figure out what the rates are going to be, ahead of time?"

He said, "That'd be amazing."

"If we knew whether the rate was going up or down, we could help customers lock in the rate they want and save them money," I offered.

After a few more minutes of kicking that idea around, Vince replied, "Marty, I don't know if the rates will go up or down, tomorrow, but I do know that they'll probably move, one way or the other."

I laughed and said, "Good point! But, there's got to be a way to figure it out."

So, I started researching interest rates: their history, what caused them, who set them, and why they were what they were.

In the process, I came across a graph published by the Federal Reserve Board. It showed the overall interest rates from July 1954 to the present.

At first, I wasn't really impressed...I thought, "Okay, well, here's a picture of all of the numbers from then 'til now."

But, as I stepped back from the graph, I started noticing little things and big things about the graph.

The first thing was that the graph made a perfect Bottom-Top-Bottom graph, over 49 years. I folded the page in half, reopened it, and almost dropped the paper on my desk!

The fold had bisected the graph, showing a equidistant "up" and "down" on the page. Freaky!

Of course, they weren't a perfect "up" and a perfect "down," but they were still there, with a peak right in the middle, as plain as day.

I turned around to show Vince, but he was on the phone.

I started waving the paper in front of him, and he started laughing, covering the mouthpiece of his desk phone, so as to not be disrespectful to the person on the other end of the line.

We had done that kind of thing to each other a number of times before, trying to see if we could get the other guy to mess up on the phone, while he was talking to somebody.

Vince finished his call, hung up, and laughingly asked, "Yes, Marty?!"

I showed him the graph, explained what I had realized, and waited for a response. He sat there quietly for a minute, staring at the graph.

All of a sudden, his jaw dropped open; his eyes got big; and he started grinning. I saw the light bulb go on in his head.

Then, he asked the question I was hoping he would ask: "So, what's it going to do next?"

What a question…the perfect question. I replied, "It's going to start all over again."

"What?"

"Sure. It's gonna repeat itself, over and over and over."

"How do you know that?"

"Because if you look at this little part, here [pointing to the graph], it looks just like this part over here."

"I'll be."

"When the Federal Reserve Board started setting the rates back in 1954, they started it at .75%. Went up for a few years, and then dropped back down to 1%...or close to where it started. Then, it took off, and ran until the early 80's, and started falling, over all, again. So, in 2004, when the rate hit 1%, again, lots of people freaked out, thinking that it would never get that low again. Well, it did, didn't it?"

"It sure did."

"So, if I'm right, the rate will continue to rise a little longer and then drop back down to 1%, or lower, because the cycle has to repeat itself – it doesn't have a choice."

"Back down to 1%? That sounds crazy, but if it does, when do you think it'll do it?"

"My guess, so far, is...by December 2007."

"The end of next year?"

"Yep."

"Well, it'll be interesting to see, at least. And if you're right, you may just be on to something."

"Let's hope so."

"What about short term?"

"Like what?"

"As in, when's the interest rate gonna drop again, so that I can close on this loan I've been working on?"

"Short term, I haven't figured out, yet, but give me some time, and I'll see what I can come up with."

Over the next couple of days, I continued to look through charts, graphs, and diagrams. I went back and looked more closely at the interest rate graph, and then, suddenly, it dawned on me – I had seen part of that graph somewhere clse!

I closed my eyes, put my fingers in my ears, and started running through the files in my head, trying to find the picture of that graph, trying to remember where I had seen it before......Nothing.

"FILE NOT FOUND" flashed across the screen in my head.

I thought, "I know it's in there – it's just a matter of remembering where."

It bugged me on the drive home. I was praying that God would help me remember where I had seen that graph, before. All evening, I kept trying to pull it out of the recesses of my mind.

My wife finally told me, "Forget about it, for a while. Do something else, to take your mind off of it, and you'll remember where you saw it. In fact, let's pull some weeds out of the flower bed – that'll take your mind off of graphs and charts."

I laughed and went outside with her. Getting some fresh air helped. Hanging out, listening to her talk about her day really helped me put aside what I was worried about (it usually does).

That night, I pulled a dozen books off of the shelf and sat down in the middle of the floor in the back room.

I started flipping through the books and notebooks, scanning the pages in an effort to find what my mind's eye saw...but where?

After a few hours of searching, I went to sleep. I hoped that maybe that would remind me of what I wanted to know.

Light Bulb During Lunch

The next day, I made my morning phone calls, worked on paperwork, and talked with Vince some more. During lunch, I sat right there at my desk, with my sandwich and drink.

It clicked! I had seen the corner of the graph in a print out that I had made from a charting site, online. I started looking back through the web site. Nothing was jumping out at me, so I began at the top and worked my way downward.

Bingo, I found it! The corner of the chart that I had recognized a day before was the same as the tail end of the Fed Funds 30-day chart. Duh!

BUT, the portion I had recognized was inverted on the new chart. How were they related? I copied and pasted the chart into Word, inverted the image, and cropped the chart, leaving only the corner.

I enlarged that bit to match the size of the paper I had printed off, the day before. Holding the two pages up to the window, I lined up the two graphs…They were identical! Incredible! I couldn't wait 'til Vince got back.

So, which came first, the chicken or the egg? I didn't really care at that point, as long as I could figure out the rest of the puzzle. Researching further, I realized that the 30-day rate closed every business day, on the commodities' market. The central bank then took that number and subtracted it from 100.

The difference became the initial interest rate to other banks, the following morning, also called the "overnight rate" by some folks. For years, many banks and loan companies charged 3% to cover their costs of doing business and to make a profit (to stay in business).

I figured, therefore, that I could take that evening's overnight rate, add the standard 3%, and come up with the next day's interest rate, ahead of time, BEFORE we got our faxed Rate Sheet, the next day.

However, after doing a few days worth of closing prices and rates, retroactively, I realized that the banks and loan companies weren't just charging 3% to cover their costs, anymore.

They were apparently charging 4-5%, depending on the institution.

I went back a little farther and saw that as the Federal Reserve (FR) rate had dropped from 4% to

3%, banks had loaned money at 7% and then 6%, respectively. But, when the FR rate had dropped from 3% to 2.5%, banks had still loaned money at 6% and continued loaning it at 6%, even as the FR rate inched its way down to 1% and then back up, again. In effect, as the banks were able to borrow money from the Central Bank at a lower rate, they did NOT pass that savings on to their borrowers.

So, instead of making a minimum of 3% per loan, they were making 3.5-5% straight off the top. That started on the ride down, but they kept it, on the way back up.

My guess, at the time, was that the banks and loan companies were trying to save up a little extra – to hold them over – in case the real estate market continued to fall and the demand for loans dried up.

Not only did I realize what was happening in the world of finance, it dawned on me that I needed to finish my lunch! I tucked away all of my papers, grabbed the last bit of my sandwich and drink, and went to go walk through the parking lot.

The day had gotten heady, from all of the realizations that had been happening in the past 24 hours! …and to think that Vince missed all of that, because he left to go eat lunch. Okay, I was a little jealous, every time he would drive away in his jet black Mercedes.

However, I will admit that he frequently reminded me that a car was still just a car, because no matter what it looked like, any one of them would get you from point A to point B. …True.

Putting It to the Test

When Vince got back, he took one look at me and asked, "What?"

The grin on my face gave something away, I guess.

"I figured it out," was my reply.

"Figured *what* out?"

"How to calculate *tomorrow's* rate sheet, *today*."

"No way!"

"Yep."

"Really? It works?"

"I'll bet you lunch."

"Okay…"

"Before we go home, today, I'll write down tomorrow's basic loan rate, and we'll lock it in your desk. If I'm right, you buy me lunch. If I'm wrong, I'll buy you lunch."

"Sounds like a deal. Either way, we'll eat something good!"

"I like the way you think!"

"So how's it work?"

I showed him the charts, explained what I had done, and explained how I thought it worked.

"And you got all that from looking at those charts?"

"Yeah, I guess so…it just clicked."

"Well, I'm glad you have a clicker in your brain."

The next morning, Vince beat me in to the office (like normal). When I got there, he was smiling from ear to ear.

"Looks like I'm buying you lunch."

"Did I get it right?"

"Dead on."

"Woooohoooo!"

At that point, the office manager came walking through, to see what all the noise was about.

We told her what I had figured out. She paused for a moment and then told us that we needed to focus on selling loans instead of predicting the rate sheet.

Vince and I looked at each other, dumbfounded. I thought she would have been ecstatic, but she wasn't really interested.

Vince and I looked back at the office manager and said, "No problem. We'll get back to making phone calls."

Vince and I sat down and started dialing. Our manager had missed the whole point, but Vince and I understood the magnitude of what we had discovered!

Beliefs vs. Reality

Later that summer, I was at a real estate workshop, learning about loan products, rates, etc. After the workshop was over, I got into a discussion with one of the trainers.

A few minutes into our discussion, his temper rose to the level of being livid with me, after I asked him what he knew about cycles.

Toward the end of our talk, he angrily said, "There's a difference between correlation and causation. I can believe in correlation, but what you're suggesting is causation!"

I said, "Yes, because if you can figure out the cause of something, then you'll have a roadmap to the future ups and downs, for the rest of your life – and for your children's lives."

At that point, the color of his face matched his bright red hair. I decided it was probably best for me to leave.

So, I thanked him for his time, smiled, and walked out to my car.

As prices dropped in 2007 and 2008, realtors told me, "Oh, but they're going to turn around next year."

I responded, "Really? What about the 18-year cycle?"

They asked, "What's that?"

I started to explain it each time, but at some point in the conversation they would get a donut look on their face (glazed over) and would look like they were a thousand miles away.

So, I would change the topic and move on. That happened time and time, again.

Likewise, it was almost comical to read articles in newspapers by people claiming that "We're through the roughest parts, and clear skies are on the horizon, so go ahead and buy a house, before prices jump up out of your range, again."

It was almost as if the newspapers were trying to create the false hope of rising prices, just to get people to buy. They were trying to create a self-fulfilling prophecy, but it didn't work.

Prices have continued to fall and will continue to do so, until this part of the cycle works itself through –

and there's nothing we can do to change that (sort of like trying to keep the moon from changing the tide from high to low, each day).

Part of what frustrates people is they that don't want to admit there are things caused in the universe that are beyond their control.

One of the biggest things I learned that summer was that people believe what they're comfortable with, even when reality and truth of the matter are telling them otherwise.

I just scratched my head, trying to understand humanity. It confused me at times, because I thought everything seemed so simple.

But, the verse Mark 8:18 came to mind, "Do you have eyes but fail to see, ears but fail to hear?" (NIV)

Ok, so some people just didn't get it.

Fine. I realized if it made sense to me and I felt compelled to share it, then I should continue to do so, even if some people didn't believe me or understand. I kept telling myself that eventually reality would play itself out through the cycles.

The cycles would have to speak for themselves. So far, they have…and right on time…

NUMBERS & DETAILS

Past Shows Where Prices Are Headed

Throughout history, real estate prices have risen and fallen, over and over and over. While prices overall have steadily risen from the beginnings of recorded history until now (due to inflation), the same can be said for just about every other thing that's bought and sold.

However, real estate differs from other things because there have been notable drops in prices, along with huge increases. And while prices have risen, the rise hasn't been in a continuous, straight line – there have been dips, rebounds, precipitous drops, and spikes.

Also, the increases and decreases in prices haven't randomly occurred – they've happened regularly and repetitively, on time, over the years. As long as you remember all of that (a snapshot in time) when you're looking at the price of real estate, you'll be fine.

Looking at the last broad top in real estate trends, prices hung around their highest points from about June 2005 until about June 2007 and then started descending rapidly. "What goes up, must come down," right?

In 1947, Edward R. Dewey and Edwin F. Dakin published a fantastic book, Cycles: The Science of Prediction.

In it, they discussed an 18.3-year cycle in real estate. They showed how the cycle played out in history and extrapolated it into the future – part of which is now our past! While no cycle is easily nailed down to an exact day and time, it's possible to get close.

Time has proven that the assessment Dewey and Dakin discussed IS accurate. People may want to disagree or argue with the cycle, but it was at work 150 years ago and is still ringing true, today.

Applying the 18.3-year idea to the dates of 2005-2007 should put the next bottom in real estate prices from around August 2014 through August 2016, with a mid-point of August 2015.

Each future bottom should occur every 18.3 years after that. Likewise, the tops should be about halfway in between each of the corresponding bottoms.

In October 2010, to tell the world what I had realized about the 18.3-year cycle, I wrote and posted and article at scribd.com/mjreep entitled,

"Next Bottom of the Real Estate Market Should Be August 2015."

As of this book's first printing, that article had only gotten 336 reads. Okay. No problem. Like my dad used to say about the fields of corn and alfalfa we planted on our farm, "We'll just have to wait and see."

I guess he's still right.

Riding the Wave or Pushing the Ocean?

Once, when I started to get frustrated with something at work, a friend asked me, "Marty, are you riding the wave or pushing the ocean?"

That made me stop and think…sure enough, I had been trying to push the ocean.

The same thing applies to trends and cycles.

Once in a while, I may want to disagree with what I see happening, but fighting against it never works. Instead, it's much safer to ride the wave than to stand in its way – and more profitable, too.

If you know that the trend is heading downward, wait it out; then, catch the next rise if you're planning on selling for a profit.

You and I can want house prices to go up or down all we want, but they do it in their own sweet time…time after time.

Shakespeare's play, "Julius Caesar," bears witness to what I'm referring to:

There is a tide in the affairs of men
Which, taken at the flood, leads on to fortune;
Omitted, all the voyage of their life
Is bound in shallows and in miseries.
On such a full sea are we now afloat,
And we must take the current when it serves,
Or lose our ventures. (Act IV, Scene ii.)

When the Bard wrote that passage, I doubt he had any hidden references to real estate in mind, but the underlying message is well-suited for many ventures.

If you've ever pursued something by taking "the current when it serves" and have been successful, you know what I'm talking about.

When real estate prices move, the trend direction moves like a tide (high or low). You can either ride it and enjoy, or you can fight against it and get extremely frustrated. Either way, the market trend will continue until it's time for it to change direction and head back the other way.

If you make your living on the ocean (fishing, diving, surfing), you learn the tide tables and live by them – meaning, you figure out when the tide is coming in and when it's going out. You'd be a fool to fight against it.

The same goes for real estate.

When you learn which way the trend is going, you work with it. When you do, you're more likely to succeed. Don't be like the people who fight against the trend and pretend like they're not. That's just like taunting a tidal wave and then trying to outrun it. It may be exciting for a few moments, but the outcome isn't very pretty.

During the last few trends in real estate, were you riding the wave or pushing the ocean? Or were you metaphorically "sitting on the beach," watching it all happen? If you were just sitting on the beach, I hope it was because you *chose* to do so and not because you were clueless about what was happening.

Even so, this book can change that in the future for you if you'll watch for key signs and apply the principles. If you're planning on buying a house at some point, use this material to help you determine when and where the real estate tide is going, so you can enjoy riding its wave.

I hope you'll be able to benefit from some of these ideas.

Understanding Interest Rates

A complete, long cycle for interest rates has proven itself to be 49 years.

To see the proof, look at a graph of the Federal Reserve Board rates from July 1954 to 2011 (Figure 1).

The data is public information from the Federal Reserve. I ran it through a spreadsheet program to show the resulting chart. Pretty eye-opening! It provides a great visual depiction of the history of rates in the U.S.

On the left side of the chart, notice how the rates started below 1%, quickly went to almost 3%, and then fell back to 1%.

Now look at the right side of the chart. Do you see a similar pattern? It's higher in the middle than the first one, but it still repeats the design.

Rates started just below 1% (.0080), went up for a few years, dropped back to below 1% (.0068), then rose again to 2%-3%.

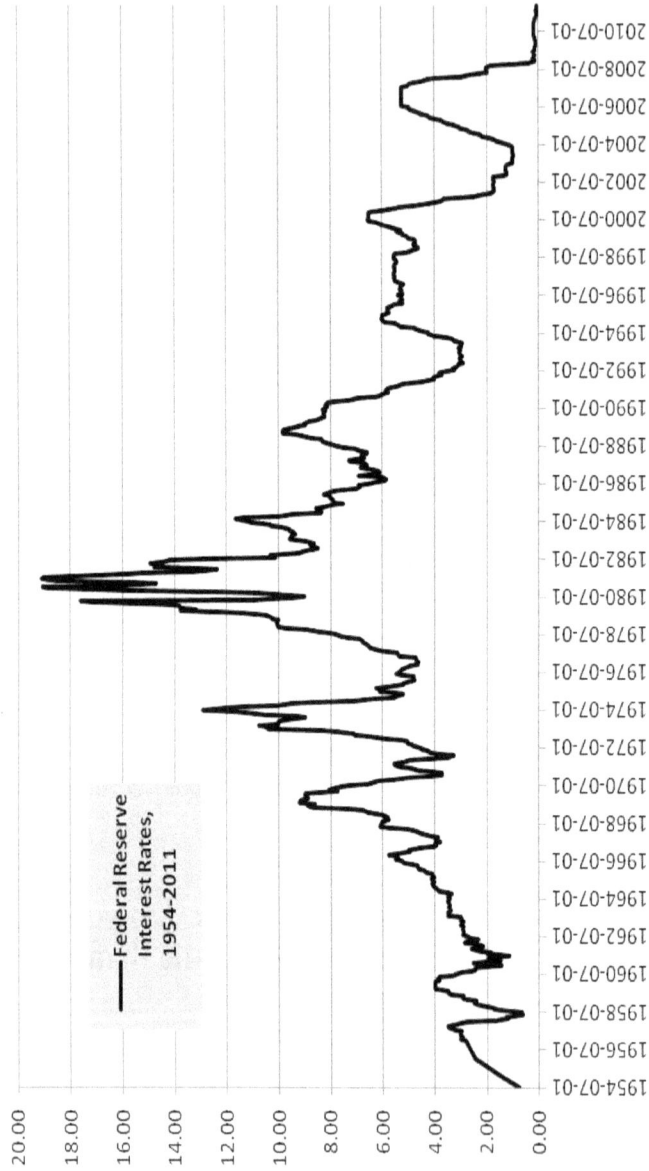

Figure 1: Interest rates showing the 49-year cycle.
Raw data from FederalReserve.gov.

After that, it moved upward until the late 1970s/early 80s, with occasional pull backs for various reasons. Ultimately, rates topped out at 19% in 1980-81.

After 1981, interest rates started heading back down to where they started: 1%. They got there in 2003, just before mid-year. That return to 1% completed the long cycle in interest rates.

What does all of this have to do with real estate cycles and prices?

A lot...

Now look at Figure 2.

While interest rates *don't cause* the real estate cycle, they *do* play a part in how high or how low prices go.

Meaning, the real estate cycle, or "wave," would exist with or without interest rates. The rates simply add energy to or take energy away from the magnitude of the wave, resulting in how high or how low the wave goes. Additionally, prices equate to the height or depth of the wave.

Notice the timing of the interest rates in relationship to the 18.3-year cycle going through them (or vice-versa).

Think back to events that played out during those various times and how much (or little) prices were affected.

Interesting?

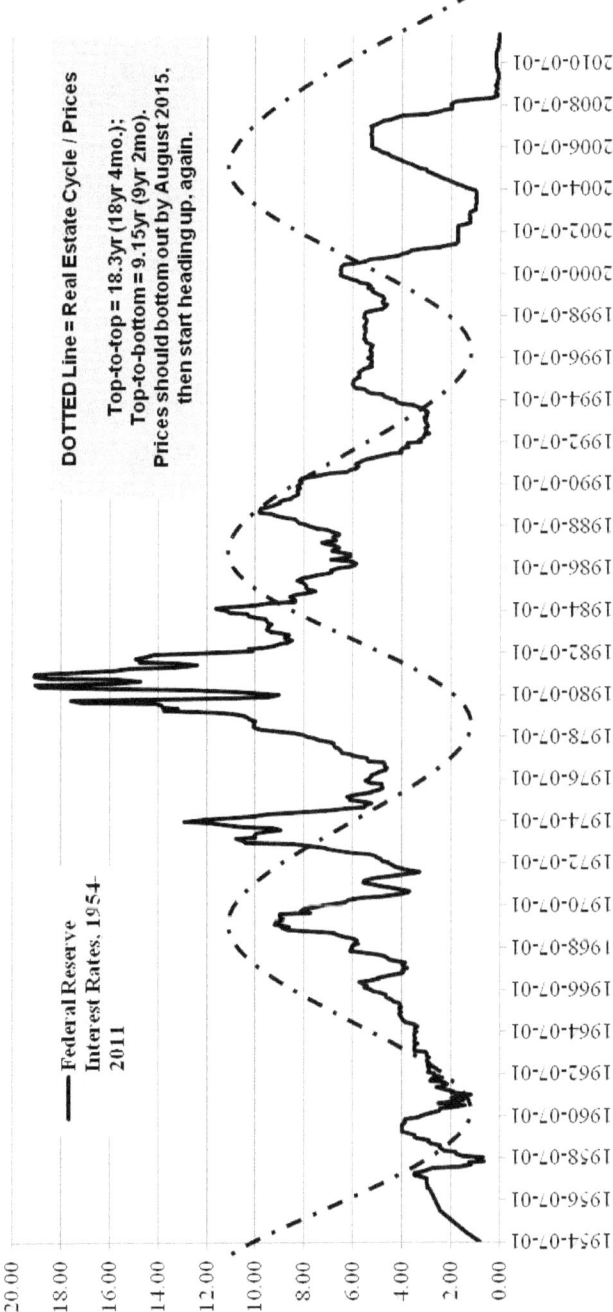

Figure 2: Interest Rates overlapped with Real Estate Cycle.

When the Federal Reserve started setting and tracking rates in 1954, the rate started just below 1%. The rate went up for a few years, and then dropped suddenly to almost 0%. The same thing happened 49 years later.

Figure 3 shows the repeating history...

While the sections of the rates graph aren't exactly the same (comparing then to now), the repeating pattern still makes itself evident.

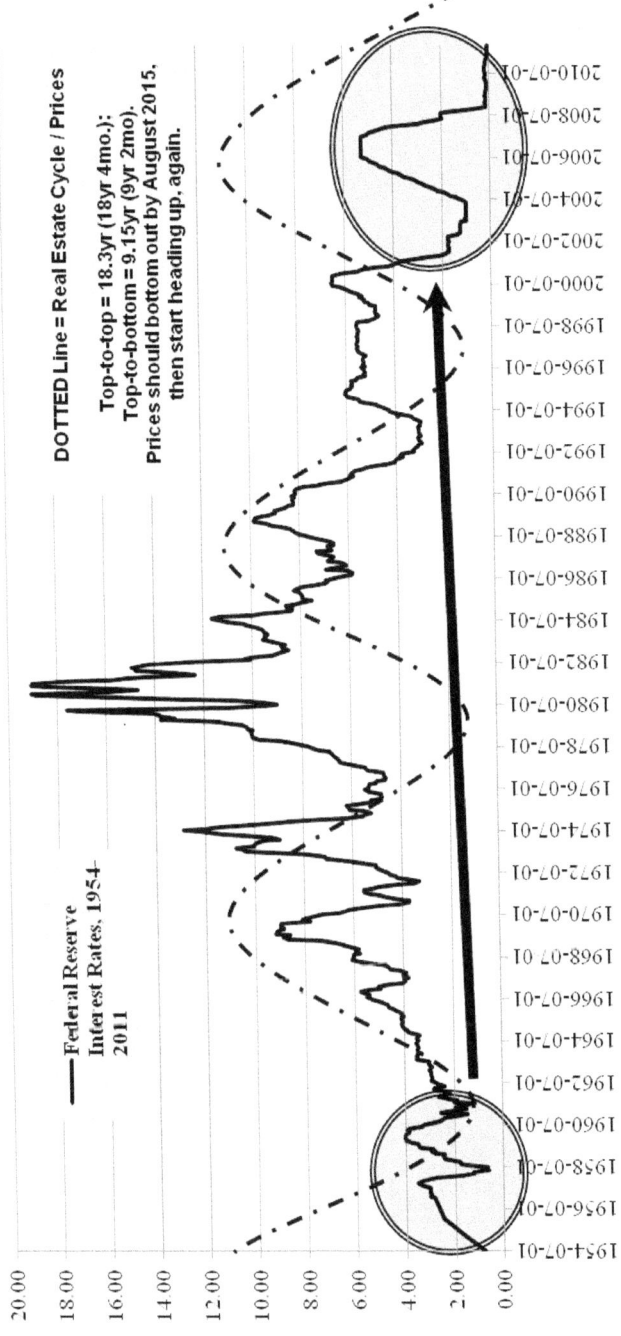

Figure 3: History repeats itself.

The Recent Real Estate Boom in the U.S.

The gigantic peaks in real estate prices from 2004-2006 in the United States was caused in part by a perfect storm of two big factors (Figure 4):

1. rising demand in real estate

and

2. falling interest rates.

Although there have been a couple of other times in our history that similar economic conditions lined up with real estate, the resulting rise in prices were never so monumental.

Because lower interest rates in years past typically meant that money was cheaper to borrow and because the laws in place at the time allowed lots of people to apply for and get real estate loans, thousands of people were flush with money to buy property. As a result, prices were pushed through the roof, and some properties doubled or tripled in price within a few years.

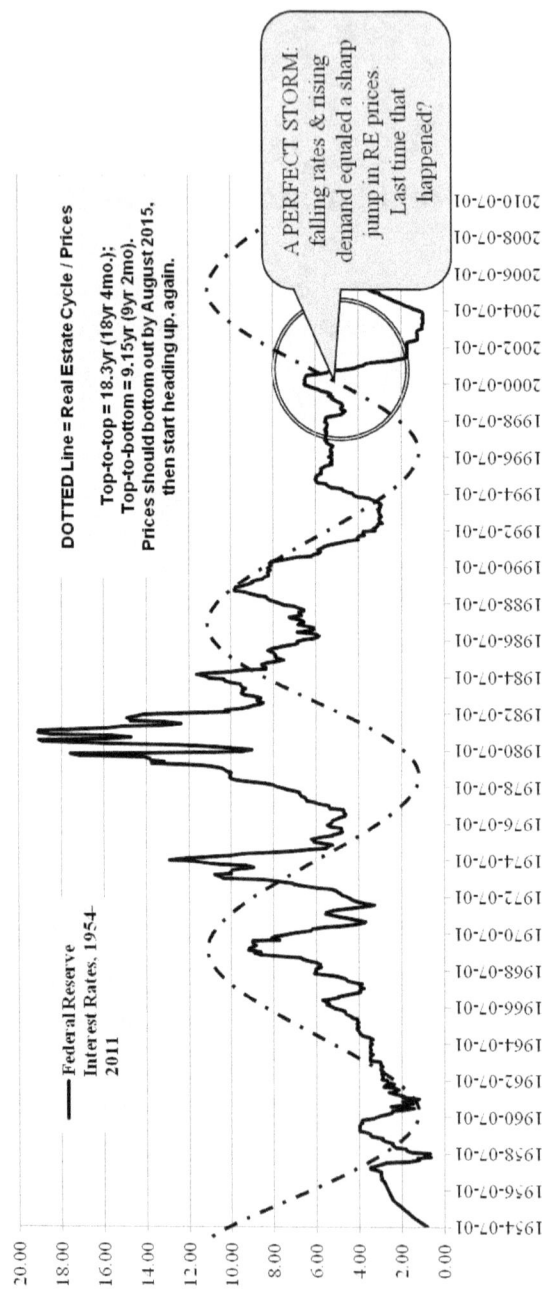

Figure 4: A Perfect Storm of Rising Demand and Falling Interest Rates.

Even realtors who had been in the business for a while said that they had never seen anything like it before. They had never seen home values climb so steeply, so fast. Likewise, they had never seen their commission checks increase so quickly, either.

During the wide top of the bubble, real estate agents and loan agents were so busy that they didn't have to go looking for new clients...clients were going to them! One loan agent told me that in 2004, she was receiving 10 applications a day to process for loans. Before that on typical days, she would receive 1 or 2 applications. She said, "It was insane. We had so much work, we couldn't get it done. 12-hour days were common, and working weekends was part of life. But, the money [commissions] was incredible."

The country had gotten real estate fever, and it seemed there was no stopping it. Every week brought new sales, new construction, and higher prices paid. Newspaper articles started running headlines like, "Is There No End?" and "Where's The Top?"

When $500,000 -$1,000,000 became the norm for family homes in California, middle-income earners started scratching their heads, asking if market prices matched reality. No, they didn't match up. But for the time being, as new properties came on the market, people submitted blind bids – they bid on properties without ever setting foot in the place – and some bid OVER the asking price! Yes, it was insanity.

Some people who sold their real estate during "the fever" made out like bandits. Overall in the country, there was a tremendous transfer of wealth. Home *buyers* signed up for 30-year mortgages and put net gains in the hands of sellers. Many sellers walked away smiling. I hope that they've invested and/or spent their capital gains well, because it'll be a while before they see that kind of real estate fever, again.

Next Low Will Be Really Low

The 18.3-year real estate cycle doesn't exist by itself, nor does it affect prices by itself. Other cycles are at work in the background, as well.

As already mentioned, the Interest Rate Cycle affects prices. As the 49-year cycle progresses through its timeline, its magnitude and force help push prices up or down, respectively.

Therefore, the next bottom in the RE cycle will probably be a lot lower than the last one, because this next one coming up:

1) will be amplified (downward) by the rise in Federal Reserve Board interest rates, which will be back up around 3%-4%, putting bank lending rates back up to 7%-8%

and

2) will be coupled with the national economic depression, which should bottom out in 2017.

Because the timing of the next bottom in real estate correlates with an ensuing rise in interest rates, fewer people will be able to borrow money than before.

If there are fewer borrowers, then there will be fewer buyers. If there are fewer buyers, then sellers will be prompted to lower their asking prices in order to make their houses affordable. Meaning, sellers will start to get nervous and drop their prices in order to entice buyers.

Like interest rate cycles running in the background scenery of real estate prices, a continued national economic downturn will lower the bottom stopping point in the demise of prices.

Because "bigger picture" economic trends recur every 80-84 years, the ugly part of the one that started in 2007 will bottom out around 2017 and then turn upward again.

Since real estate prices and the overall U.S. economic trend are both heading downward, one seemingly adds force to the other. That means that real estate prices will have to suffer through the effects of a Greater Depression before they turn around.

In fact, the famous market trader, W.D. Gann, used to talk about "cycles within cycles." What we've been discussing in this chapter is a prime example of that very thing.

Next Rise Won't Be as High as Last One

Just as a rise in interest rates will indirectly extend the upcoming low in the real estate cycle, the rise in interest rates will also lessen the height of the next top.

The rise in rates will make it more expensive for people to borrow money over the course of loan, so the market will react in part, by prices staying lower than they went during the last bubble.

Based on the timing of the next top in real estate prices – in conjunction with the interest rates of that time period – the next top will only rise to 2/3 of the last top.

In other words, if a house peaked at $600k last time, it will only go back up to $400k next time. Or if a house peaked at $90k, it'll only go back up to $60k during the next frenzy of price jumps.

At the time of the next real estate price peak, the USA will be coming out of the Greater Depression (the cycle that runs in 80-84 year increments). As a result, most people's net worth will still be recovering from a national financial battering that the majority of people will have never seen the likes of before. Couple that with the other two factors of the equation (lower demand with higher interest rates), and you'll still get a peak – but lower than the one in 2006.

So, What IS a Cycle?

A cycle is basically a repetition of an event or series events. Most have a beginning, a middle, and an end. Some series of events can take a long time to repeat, while others will only take a short time.

When lots of cycles happen, one after another, you get a pattern or "history." One of the most commonly known cycles is the lunar cycle, or the phases of the moon that we see. Since the positions of the Earth, the moon, and the sun (in relation to each other) are constantly changing, the appearance of the shape of the moon changes. The moon, itself, stays the same shape, but what we are able to see, changes.

Those repeating changes form a cycle. Every 28 days (on average), the cycle begins, again. Because people were able to depend on the repetition of the lunar cycle throughout history, they were able to form calendars and "time calculators," thus being able to project events and occurrences forward and backwards in time.

Events or actions that repeat on schedule can be used to verify the past and to calculate the future.

In looking at the past with a focus on cycles, we can determine patterns and averages that can be applied to the future in order to see what lies ahead.

Why Cycles Should Matter to You

If you understand what cycles are and when they happen, you can anticipate them. If you can anticipate them, then you can figure out how to benefit or profit from them. One purpose of profiting from them would be to improve your life and the lives of your family and friends. Basically, if you knew when the market was rising or falling, you would be able to time your buying and selling for maximum returns on your investments.

Real estate market prices will continue to cycle through their ups and downs whether you or I do anything. They were set in motion at the beginning of time and will continue long after we're dead and gone. But while we're alive, we can learn the cycles and benefit from them.

Telling you how to hit the exact top or exact bottom of the market is NOT one of my intentions. However, if you ever do hit one of the tops or bottoms exactly, then that could be an added bonus for you. *But, again, that's not the intention of this information.*

My intent is to help you understand the broader scope of cycles and to be able to recognize the trends of prices in your local market(s). If you learn how to do that and can benefit in different ways, then I'll be quite happy.

Learning to *SEE* the patterns of your local real estate market is sort of like having a blindfold taken off of your eyes.

For example, have you ever driven in the fog? If so, you've probably thought, "I know there's stuff in front of me and on both side of the road, but I just can't see it clearly."

Real estate prices might have seemed like that before reading this information, but by the time you finish, hopefully the fog will lift, and you'll be able to see clearly in front of you and around you.

Signs of a Rising Market

1. Lots of people become agents:

Around 2002 or 2003, as RE prices continued to rise, I noticed that more and more people were getting their RE agent's license. In talking to a friend, who had been an agent for a number of years, I asked her what she thought. She said she was glad to see prices moving back up (after being down for so long) and was glad there was interest in the local market, again.

What that means and what to look for:

She said that with so many new people becoming agents, there were bound to be issues that came up: paperwork omissions, loan mishaps, misrepresentations, etc. Because of that, she recommended that when it came time to buy or sell a house, I should pick someone who had years of experience. Of course, she was trying to protect and grow her own business, but she had a point. At that time, she had been an agent for ten years. Later, as the market continued to rise and grow, she benefited from the bubble – selling lots of houses. Yet after the crash, she stayed in the business, continuing to help clients. Today, she's still a RE agent – I think it's in her blood. As far as experience goes, she definitely has it.

2. Real Estate is talked about, more and more, in the news:

For years, I was hard-pressed to find regular articles in the newspaper about real estate. Once the market started heating up, though, almost every newspaper had regular articles about some aspect of real estate: how to buy, how to sell, where to look, interest rates, forecasts, etc. Web sites dedicated whole sections to just those topics. Huge chunks of time and space were dedicated to RE. Suddenly, everybody was an expert.

What that means and what to look for:

When a market becomes saturated with commentary, people can become desensitized to the information. Some just tune it out and stop listening. That's when people get hurt: if they miss the signs of changes in the market, they wind up getting swept up and carried away by the underlying, driving forces. Purpose and intent can get lost in the words, unless you keep yourself awake to market trigger words that you need to hear, in order to get in and out at the most opportune times. The point is to not just take information at face value. Weigh it against what you know to be true, what you see going on around you in your neighborhood, and what your gut tells you to be correct. Yes, there are experts in the field of real estate, just like there are experts in every other profession and marketplace. But, not everyone is an expert. Some people are just guessing. Lots of hype doesn't always mean the information is true, nor does it always mean the information is false. Just know that when it seems that almost everyone is talking about something, then "mass psychology" is on the move and can indicate that problems are about to happen on a large scale.

How Laws Added to the Housing Crash

During the past few decades, real estate lending laws governing Fannie Mae and Freddie Mac were relaxed. Homebuyers and investors were able borrow large amounts of money – larger than ever before – at lower and lower interest rates.

As the prices of homes rose, the loans on them also rose, increasing the amount of money that was "promised" and "lent on the street." Many people went with an adjustable-rate mortgage since it would keep their monthly payments lower than a fixed-rate mortgage would. However, some of those borrowers would find out the hard way what happens when rates start rising – it would "adjust" them out of their homes.

Likewise, underwriters were encouraged to ease their guidelines and allow more loans that didn't require all of the typical proof-of-income documents – known as 'No Doc' loans. That made it easier for more people to borrow "cheap" money, which in turn pushed home prices higher.

Everything seemed to be floating smoothly along, until house prices started falling, and then suddenly the magic formula didn't work anymore.

Homeowners and investors became financially upside down, started missing payments, and started defaulting on their loans. When that happened, banks started losing money, and the whole thing unraveled.

The Next 80 Years

At this point, you may be wondering what the long-term future looks like with the 18.3-year real estate cycle. Based on the averages of past ups and downs, it should play out something like this:

Low – August 2015
High – October 2024
Low – December 2033
High – February 2043
Low – April 2052
High – June 2061
Low – August 2070
High – October 2079

There it is...short and sweet, but to the point.

Obviously, you may not be around for some of the upcoming dates...those would be to share with your kids and grandkids...

PROFITING FROM YOUR NEW KNOWLEDGE

Benefiting from the Trends

Investing in anything, especially real estate, should not be done without consulting the advice of professionals. Even then, it's still just that: advice. YOU have to make the final choice in what you're going to do with your energy, time, and money. Be deliberate; be careful; and choose wisely.

Educate yourself before jumping into anything. Like Benjamin Franklin used to say, "If a man empties his purse into his head, no one can take it from him."

Also, if you miss the rise or fall of one cycle, don't worry, it'll be back – you can catch the next one. It's not like real estate is going to disappear…because if it did, then we'd have much bigger problems to deal with than the timing of cycles!

Because it takes some cycles so many years to coincide with one another, I will most likely be long gone (dead) before the next recurrence of "the perfect storm" happens. That's why I've taught my kids how to calculate the collisions of cycles – their children will be living when those cycles will coincide. I feel like I've prepped my family on how to profit from the bigger, long term cycles and how to avoid some the pitfalls that I learned from, the hard way. When all of those thoughts and ideas run through my head, the verse, Proverbs 13:22a comes to mind: "A good man leaves an inheritance for his children's children...." This book is one way of honoring the intent of that verse.

Part of the trouble with long cycles is that after one comes around in your favor, you may not live long enough to enjoy its opportunities, again. So, one way to benefit from future long cycles is to pass on your knowledge and experiences to your children, grandchildren, or somebody else who is of a future generation.

Knowing something that could change the world and keeping it to yourself is not in the equation for success. Part of the reason that we learn things and are allowed to realize their significance is so that we'll share them with others. Still, some things we learn are for us to keep to ourselves; therefore, you'll have to weigh out the pros and cons to determine what you're supposed to do with what you know and learn.

Profiting from Falling Prices

People often ask, "How do you make money in a falling real estate market?"

After watching the rise and fall of prices locally and around the country, here are a few different approaches that have come up:

1) **Buy a foreclosure.** Foreclosures can give you a chance to pick up property at a discount. Currently, there are numerous foreclosures on the market. Depending on where you live, there could be a handful, dozens, or even hundreds of foreclosures for sale in your area. Foreclosure laws vary by state, and each lender has its own set of regulations and procedures for buying property. So, find out what they are for the property you're interested in, and get moving!

2) **Buy a short sale.** Short sales are similar to foreclosures in that they're typically sold at a discount. They're different (in part) because of the rules involved in buying.

3) **Buy "regular" property near the bottom of the market.** Now that you know when the market should bottom out *(from the research I discussed in previous chapters)*, you can follow real estate in your local area and buy when it's priced right for you.

4) **Hold on to what you already have.** Ride out the falling market, and then sell for a profit when prices rise. Prices won't bounce back immediately, but they will bounce back over time. It comes down to a matter of how long you can hold on, until the market heads back in your favor.

As with any piece of real estate, how you go about watching and buying depends on your intent.

What do you plan to do with the property if you get it?

- Hold on to it forever?
- Hold it for a number of years?
- Develop it?
- Improve it?
- Flip it?

All of your answers will shape your plan of attack in profiting from falling and rising prices.

The price of your home is irrelevant, as long as you like where you live and/or can afford the payments. Prices rise and fall over and over, but the only time that the market price of your home should concern you is when/if you plan to put in on the market.

Otherwise, the numbers in the news don't really matter…..Think about it.

Momentum Is Powerful

In the stock market, a saying that's been around a while is, "Bulls make money; bears make money; and hogs get slaughtered." The same applies to real estate. You can make money in a rising market by selling houses for more than you paid. You can make money in a falling market by holding on through the drop and renting out your investment houses until the prices come back around. Another way to profit in a falling market is to buy houses that the banks and loan companies have in their inventory. They want to get rid of that inventory, so they will sell at a loss, in order to be able to lend more money.

But, if you hold out for the top of the real estate market, trying to sell at the very peak, you could wind up having to stick it out until the next rise in prices. Therefore, greedy people (a.k.a. "hogs") get slaughtered in the market.

Momentum is a powerful force. Part of the reason that people get slaughtered when prices near a top, is because they wind up buying in the midst of a surge of national momentum, get carried over the peak, and are taken down the other side. When prices near a bottom or a top, the tide of momentum does funny things. It messes with people's psyche. I've seen people bid more for houses than they should have, simply because of the sweeping force of momentum. They knew better, but they didn't want to be left out of making the "easy money" that everybody talked about, in real estate.

People get swept away when momentum is the driving force of the moment. Could they fight against it? Like I've said before, "They could…" but they'd just wind up tired. A better solution would be to step aside and avoid the momentum, altogether. Simply remove yourself from the situation and watch the action from the sidelines. If you've ever lost a lot of money, you know that being greedy doesn't work well…especially when momentum is involved.

At the same time, the power of momentum can carry you to great heights. You can ride a national trend and profit nicely. Some friends of mine sold while the market was rising, and they made a handsome profit. They turned around and bought another house, fixed it, and did the same thing. Then, they stopped buying and just sat on their profits. Once the nationwide frenzy stopped, they waited for prices to cool down, before buying the house they planned on retiring in. They didn't know just how much prices were going to fall, though, so adding the profits they made to the later drop in prices, they paid cash for the house they're in, now. A success story in the midst of a surge of energy.

Momentum…I also remember watching house prices rise in my neighborhood in 2002, 2003, and 2004. As the tide of excitement rose in real estate, houses sold for thousands more, every month. A house down at the corner sold for $10k over asking price, sight-unseen. Sight unseen?! (That's like "buying a pig in a poke" – you don't know what you're getting until you take it home and open the sack).

Yet, the folks who bought it are still there and seem to be happy. In the same breath, I know of a number of people who bought too late in the upswing, financially overextended themselves, and lost their home. Hard lessons learned, but still a lesson. Most of them are doing okay, though.

My point? Be aware of the power of momentum. Don't ignore it. Use it to benefit you in your endeavors.

Cash Will Be King, Again

One of the results of a credit crunch and depressed market will be that cash will be king, again. Just like many times in the past, people will be less concerned about perceived equity in a property and more concerned about liquidity.

Having enough cash on hand to buy and close on a property will mean that you control the transaction. You'll be able to get better terms than other people. You'll also have a better selection of properties to choose from than other potential buyers.

If you're able to walk into a deal offering all cash or a substantial amount of the price, you'll be in a strong position. With cash, you'll also be able to negotiate a better deal than with little or no cash.

MARTY'S RULES

7 Rules

for

Profiting from Trends

Rule #1 – Don't bet your home.

Some lessons are gained the easy way (learning them from other people's mistakes), but most are gained the hard way (learning them from our own mistakes). Betting your home may seem like a sure-fire source of investment capital, but when a high-priced market drops suddenly, like it did in 2006, your nest egg may get fried. Aside from causing unnecessary financial risk, betting your home in speculative investments can cause stress, weaken relationships, and keep you awake at night. Nobody needs that, so, *"Don't bet your home."*

Rule #2 – Invest in a familiar market.

If you live in St. Louis, the housing market in Houston is most likely out of your immediate area, unless you have business interests that take you there, regularly. For example, a friend of mine who lives in the Central Coast of California sells water systems for large buildings, so he frequently travels to Las Vegas, a week at a time. Although Vegas is almost 300 miles from his home, that could be an appropriate market for him to invest in, because he's there, a lot. On the other hand, any other city 300 miles away would be out of his "known zone," so he'd be wise to steer clear. So, *"Invest in a market you're familiar with."*

Rule #3 – Do a gut check.

Have you ever started to do something but felt uneasy about it, in your gut? That's your mind, your body, your soul, common sense, and/or the universe telling you, "WAIT!" – and you'd be pretty smart to find out why. If your gut is telling you to investigate further, there's a reason you're sensing that resistance or uneasiness.

Likewise, have you ever started to do something and felt completely confident about moving forward with your plans? Then, that's the right thing to do. Follow through on it with confidence and gusto. God made us with internal checks and balances…we just have to slow down and get quiet enough to listen. So, *"Do a gut check."*

Rule #4 – Ask for help.

Men and women are different when it comes to asking for help. We just are…it's the way God made us. So, men, here's an area where we can learn from women: "Ask for help." Instead of just running full speed into the dark unknown, stop and ask for directions. I know, that's blasphemy in some circles…but I get tired of driving around, lost, and winding up the wrong neighborhoods, again and again!

After about the third or fourth time that it happened after I got married, I decided that trips would be much more fun if I just stopped and asked somebody for help. Okay, the directions we get sometimes aren't always perfect, but if they don't work out exactly right, at least I have a scapegoat! Right?… I'm just sayin'. So, *"Ask for help."*

Rule #5 – Pull the trigger.

Once you've researched your market, followed the trend, and figured out when's right for you, then "pull the trigger." So many people that I've known, over the years, have been afraid to *act*. Oh sure, they were great at analyzing things and talking about doing something …someday, but they never carried through on it. Some of them may very well still be sitting in the same place, stuck in contemplation constipation mode. Healthy fear can save your life – I'm not talking about that. What I'm referring to is the analysis paralysis that people get stuck in, to the point that they never actually do something about what they've prepared for. After you prepare, DO something, otherwise you'll still be frustrated. When the time is right, you'll know. To move forward, you have to DO something positive, for good reasons. So, *"Pull the trigger."*

Rule #6 – Be proactive.

Stop waiting for the world to come to your doorstep and drop success in your lap. It ain't gonna happen. Some people whine about not succeeding in life, yet sit there, watching another sitcom on TV. That's sort of like expecting a car to work without putting gas in and driving it. If you want to succeed in life, you have to be proactive. Research your market; watch the prices; look back at history, and see where trends have carried a neighborhood, a city, or a state. Look up data and charts online, and talk to people. You'd probably be really amazed at how smart some people are, where you live – and if you're amiable, they'd probably love to share what they know, with you. Get out there, and drum up business for yourself…let people know what you do and why you do it. People want to help. So, *"Be proactive."*

Rule #7 – Believe you can succeed!

My mom and dad used to tell me that I could be anything I wanted to be, in life, and that if I tried hard enough, I would succeed. They were right. Success hasn't always come in the ways I expected, nor in my timelines, but it has arrived, just as it should have. Overall, it did not disappoint. In fact, some things were more successful than I ever imagined, in ways I didn't expect. Yet, in the final analysis, success came. Therefore, I encourage you to pursue your dreams; fight for what is right; challenge your own inconsistencies; and face your fears. You can overcome all obstacles – they might seem insurmountable, but they're really not. As you challenge the status quo, you will see hindrances fall away. The road will open up to you, and your vision will become clear. One day, you will awaken to find that life is more than you ever imagined it could be. So, *"Believe you can succeed!"*

We each live life once,
but if lived right,
once is enough…

Live it well.

EPILOGUE

So, what's next for you? Whatever your goals are, regarding real estate cycles, I encourage you to go out there and do them! If you want to buy a house and sell it, then go for it. If you want to buy a house and keep it to live in, then do that. If you want to watch and wait, to see if the market really will cycle through the way that I'm predicting in this book, then that's okay, too.

Either way, do what's right for your situation. Not everyone is in the same financial place, so other people may respond differently than you do to the information presented here. The main thing is to figure out what makes sense for you and to follow through on it.

As you go forward with your newfound knowledge and understanding in the world of real estate, I'd love to hear how you're doing. If you care to, send me a note at the email address found on this book's copyright page.

Until then, may your life continue to be enriched!

   ~ Marty

SOURCES

Dewey, Edward R. and Edwin F. Dakin. <u>Cycles: the Science of Prediction</u>. New York: H. Holt and Company, 1947.

Federal Reserve. Historical Federal Funds Rate. federalreserve.gov.

Federal Reserve Bank of St. Louis. Historical Federal Funds Rate. research.stlouisfed.org.

Reep, Marty J. "Next Bottom of the Real Estate Market Should Be August 2015." <u>www.scribd.com/mjreep</u> . Posted October 2010.

Shakespeare, William. "Julius Caesar." Act IV. Scene ii.

Thomas, Vince. Multiple discussions, 2006-2012.

OTHER BOOKS BY MARTY

Motivational / Self Help
Believe. Do. and Follow Through! (Amazon.com)

Poetry
Morning Coffee (Amazon.com)
Letting In, Letting Out (Amazon.com)
Making Sense of It All (Scribd.com)

Children's Books
Snail Parade / El Desfile de los Caracoles (Amazon.com)
      (English/Spanish)
Winston T. Mouse / Winston T. Ratón (Amazon.com)
      (English/Spanish)
Winston T. Mouse / オアエサヂエ T/ ミォサ(Scribd.com)
      (English/Japanese)
Winston T. Mouse / Winston T. Tikus (Scribd.com)
      (English/Indonesian)
Winston T. Topo / Winston T. Mouse (Scribd.com)
      (Italian/English)
Winston T. Maus / Winston T. Mouse (Scribd.com)
      (German/English)

Blog
Raised By A Village